Freezer Meals for a Cooler Life

The Secrets to a Stress-Free Life in the Kitchen

Disclaimer

Effort has been made to ensure that the information in this book is accurate and complete. However, the author and the publisher do not warrant the accuracy of the information, text and graphics contained within the book due to the rapidly changing nature of science, research, known and unknown facts. The author and the publisher do not hold any responsibility for errors, omissions or contrary interpretation of the subject matter herein. This book is presented solely for motivational and informational purposes only.

Other Books by Morgan White

Table of Contents

Freezing Meals...For What?

Freezing meals has a lot of advantages.

Just to start it's incredible how much money you can save buying foods in bulk!

Imagine you receive unexpected visits. Now what? Easy: just reheat one of your already extra tasty frozen meals!

If you're anything like me you probably hate cooking every single night. Now you don't have to: with some planning in advance you will only have to cook 2-3 nights a week. It really is a stress reliever!

The thing I enjoy the most about freezing meals is the better lifestyle it gives me. I'm not just talking about the money saving, although that's important for sure. I'm talking about getting home from work, after a stressful day, and be able to lie down on my favorite couch and know that I won't have to prepare any meal for that day.

If you're a lady just imagine: getting home, doing your nails and watching your favorite TV show while enjoying a glass of wine.

Or if you're a guy, like me, picture this: grabbing a cold one, heading for the living room and just chill while watching your favorite sport. Hmm, sounds good to me!

Tips You Should Know

Most ingredients, when frozen, can last from 1-2 months up to 4 months. Some even go as far as 12 months. I'm not telling you this for testing those limits but to show you the considerable window of opportunity you have to prepare those tasty meals.

Usually whole cuts of uncooked meat or large pieces of whole cuts will last more in the freezer than small pieces.

Air around the food isn't helpful at all, so you should seal the ingredients the best you can.

Foods that freeze well: seafood, fish, meat, bread, soups, stews, stock, most vegetables, cheese, ham, bacon, ginger, fresh chili, horseradish, pastry, cooked rice, berries, bananas and herbs.

Foods that <u>don't</u> freeze well: tomato, celery, spinach, lettuce, cucumber, lettuce, most dairy products (except cheese), raw potatoes, mayonnaise and cream sauces, whole eggs and jam.

Although freezing food slows down harmful bacteria, it doesn't kill it, so avoid refreezing raw food or any food for that matter.

In the beginning I would forget which frozen meal was in each container. <u>Not anymore:</u> get yourself a sharpie and painters tape and mark all containers with the cooking instructions and the date you made it.

You cooked something and it's still hot or, at least, warm. What should you do? Let it cool completely before freezing it.

Before eating thaw the ingredients, or the meals, in the refrigerator for 12-24 hours. Make sure you put it on a plate that can contain leaks.

About Bulk Buying

Once you get the hang of freezing meals (and feel the improvement on the quality of your life) you will probably think about getting an extra freezer. You can find some good ones in the $100-$200 range of price.

Once you start looking for bulk buying options you will probably come to the same conclusions than me:

- Products in season are cheaper and tastier.

- Meats on large packages are cheaper.

- Some warehouse clubs or grocery stores lower the price of some categories of ingredients always at the same period of time (example: week to week, or every second week). Learn about it and buy those particular ingredients in big quantities during those days.

- You will discover that some products are cheaper online, so give it a try.

My favorite options for storing things in the freezer are plastic deli containers, zip-lock bags and aluminum foil pans. You can use them multiple times and, because they are very affordable you won't feel bad when you need to get rid of them.

Conversions

1 cup = 237 ml (milliliters)

1 teaspoon = 5 ml

1 tablespoon = 15 ml = 3 teaspoons

1 Oz (liquids) = 30 ml

8 Oz (liquids) = 1 cup

1 Oz = 28 grams

1 inch = 2.54 cm (centimeters)

1lb. = 454 gr. (grams)

1 quart = 946 ml

4 cups = 1 quart

1 pint = 550 ml

Chicken Freezer Meals

Chicken Black Bean Chili

Serving: 6

Preparation time: 5 min.

Cooking time: 30 min.

Ingredients:

- 4 chicken breasts, cooked and shredded
- 40 oz. tomato sauce
- 30 oz. black beans, drained and rinsed
- 2 diced shallots
- 2 teaspoons garlic powder
- 4 teaspoons chili powder
- 2 teaspoons cumin
- 1 teaspoon red pepper flakes

Preparation method:

1. Combine all ingredients in a bowl and toss to coat chicken well.

Freezing method:

1. Place ingredients in a zip-lock bag and shake once again to coat the chicken.

2. Set in the freezer and keep until ready to use.

Cooking method:

1. Set the chicken in the refrigerator overnight to thaw.

2. Place all ingredients in the large pot or sauce pan and cook for 30 minutes.

3. Serve while still hot.

Chicken Pie

Serves: 6

Preparation time: 10 min.

Cooking time: 1 hour

Ingredients:

- 2 chicken breasts, cooked and shredded
- 1 cup broccoli florets
- 1 cup chopped carrots
- ½ cup corn
- 1 teaspoon onion powder
- 1 teaspoon garlic powder
- 1 teaspoon salt
- Fresh ground pepper – to taste
- 1 package pie crust – by your choice

Preparation method:

1. Place all ingredients in a bowl and toss to combine well.

2. Place in zip-lock bag and set in freezer.

Freezing method:

1. Lay the zip-lock bag to freezer, in flat position.
2. Freeze and keep until ready to use.

Cooking method:

1. Set the prepared mixture into refrigerator overnight to thaw.
2. Preheat oven to 180C/350F and grease pie pan with some oil. Roll out the two pie crust between 2 pieces parchment paper and place one on the bottom.
3. Place thawed ingredients in the prepared pie crust and cover with other crust. Pinch firmly to seal the edges and place in the preheated oven.
4. Bake for 1 hour and slice when cooled slightly.

NOTE: You can make the pie completely and freeze it that way, and after just bake at 180C/350F again for 1 hour.

Chicken Bites with Pineapple

Serves: 6

Preparation time: 15 min.

Cooking time: 8 min.

Reheating time: 20 min.

Ingredients:

- 1 lb. chicken, cut into bite sizes
- 1 cup all-purpose flour
- 3 tablespoons cornstarch
- 3 eggs
- Large pinch of salt
- Some vegetable oil – to fry

For the sauce:

- 14 oz. pineapple, diced, with juice
- ½ onion, finely chopped
- ½ cup water

- ½ green pepper, chopped
- ½ teaspoon salt
- 3 tablespoons apple cider vinegar
- 2 tablespoons cornstarch
- 2 tablespoons sugar

Preparation method:

1. Preheat oil in the Dutch oven on medium heat.
2. In a large bowl combine salt, flour and cornstarch.
3. Make a well in the center and crack in the eggs and add water.
4. Whisk well until you have smooth mixture and add sliced chicken; stir to coat well.
5. Using a fork drop chicken bites in the heated oil and cook for 3 minutes.
6. Set on paper towel to cool and drain.

Preparing the sauce:

1. Heat some oil in the sauce pan and cook onion, until starting to softened.

2. Add canned pineapple, sugar, vinegar and salt. Bring to a boil.
3. Combine the cornstarch and water in a separate bowl or cup until dissolved. Add to pineapple mixture along with green pepper. Simmer 2 minutes until thick.

Freezing method:

1. Place chicken bites in one zip-lock bag and sauce in other.
2. Place in the freezer, flat position and keep until ready to use.

Reheating method:

1. Soak zip-lock bag in bowl of hot water, for 6-8 minutes.
2. Preheat oven to 180C/350F and line baking tray with parchment paper.
3. Arrange chicken bites onto baking sheet and bake for 15-20 minutes or until crisp.
4. Sauce: set the sauce in the freezer overnight to thaw.

5. Place the sauce in sauce pan and heat over medium heat for 10 minutes.
6. Serve over chicken while still hot.

Chicken Croquettes

Serves: 6

Preparation time: 50 min.

Cooking time: 3 minutes

Ingredients:

- 2 ½ lb. chicken meat, preferably drumsticks
- 3 garlic cloves
- 6 tablespoons butter
- 2 eggs
- 1 cup breadcrumbs
- Fresh ground salt and pepper
- 1 onion, chopped
- ¾ cup flour
- ½ cup vegetable oil
- 1 large sweet potato, or 2 small
- 1/3 cup chicken stock

Preparation method:

1. Preheat oven to 220C/425F and line baking tray with aluminum foil.
2. Arrange chicken drumsticks onto baking tray and rub all over with two tablespoons butter.
3. Season with salt and pepper, add whole garlic cloves and wrap with the foil.
4. Bake for 45 minutes and set on wire rack to cool. Discard the skin and bones, and shred chicken meat finely.
5. Meanwhile stab the potato several times and place in the microwave; cook for 8-10 minutes. Peel the potato and place in the bowl; add reserved baked garlic and mash until you have fine puree.
6. In small sauce pan melt the remaining butter, over medium heat and add onion. Cook until softened, for 6-8 minutes.
7. Stir in ¼ cup flour and cook, stirring constantly, for 3 minutes. Gradually add the chicken stock and cook for 3 minutes more, stirring occasionally.
8. Combine prepared paste with the mashed potato and stir in shredded chicken; season with salt and pepper.

9. Whisk the eggs in a bowl, place breadcrumbs in the shallow plate and do the same with remaining butter.
10. Form the croquettes from the prepared mixture and roll them in the flour, eggs and in breadcrumbs. Repeat the process until you have no mixture left.

Freezing process:

1. Place the prepared croquettes in the food container and freeze until ready to use.

Cooking method:

1. Place the container with frozen croquettes in a bowl with hot water, for 5 minutes, just to separate them easily, if they stick to each other.
2. Heat vegetable oil in the deeper frying pan and cook croquettes for 1 ½ minute per side or until nicely golden.
3. Set on paper towel to drain and optionally serve with some lemon wedges.

Chicken Casserole

Serves: 6

Preparation time: 10 min.

Cooking time: 50 min.

Ingredients:

- 3 ½ lb. chicken breasts, cut into large pieces
- 3 tablespoons olive oil
- 2 lb. chunky vegetables – broccoli, cauliflower, bell peppers, cherry tomatoes
- 1 ½ cups chicken stock
- 1 ½ tablespoon dried thyme
- 3 tablespoons flat-leaf parsley, chopped
- 3 ¾ cups condensed cream of chicken soup
- Fresh ground salt and pepper – to taste

Preparation method:

1. Heat olive oil in non-stick pan, over medium heat and fry the chicken until slightly brown on the edges.
2. Add the thyme, stock and cream soup and mix.
3. Stir in vegetables and bring to boil. Season with salt and pepper; set aside to cool.

Freezing method:

1. You can freeze the chicken in casseroled dish or in the zip-lock bag.
2. Place in the freezer, flat position and keep until ready to use.

Cooking method:

1. Place the casserole mixture into refrigerator overnight, to thaw.
2. Place the prepared chicken in the casserole dish and bake for 45 minutes. Garnish with the chopped parsley before serving.

Seafood

Freezer Meals

Freezer Shrimps with Cabbage

Serves: 6

Preparation time: 10 min.

Cooking time: 20 min.

Reheating time: 50 sec.

Ingredients:

- 4 lb. shrimps, cleaned
- 4 stick butter, soften at room temperature
- ¾ cup white wine
- ½ cup minced shallots
- 3 egg yolks
- 1/3 cup chopped flat-leaf parsley
- 1 ½ cup bread crumbs
- Fresh ground salt and pepper
- 1 ½ teaspoons red pepper flakes
- 10 garlic cloves, minced

- 2 lemons, juice and zest

Cabbage side dish:

- 3 cups shredded cabbage, green or red
- 1 tablespoon vegetable oil
- 1 jalapeno or chili pepper, thinly sliced
- Fresh ground salt

Preparation method:

1. Place softened butter in the food processor; add bread crumbs, scallions, parsley, egg yolks, salt, pepper, minced garlic, lemon juice, lemon zest, and red pepper flakes.
2. Transfer to the large bowl and add cleaned shrimps.
3. Toss to coat the shrimps well and let it for 10 minutes.
4. Meanwhile prepare the cabbage; heat vegetable oil in large pan and when hot add the cabbage.
5. Sauté for 5-7 minutes and season with salt and pepper.

6. Set aside to cool as well.

Freezing method:

1. Place the coated shrimps in the food containers and top with butter mixture; set in the freezer; keep until ready to use.
2. Place the cabbage in freezer bags and keep in the freezer up to 1 week.

Cooking method:

1. Place the shrimps in the refrigerator overnight to thaw. Do the same with cabbage.
2. Preheat the oven to 200C/400F and place the shrimps with butter in oven safe baking trays. You will need two. Pour over the white wine and place in the oven.
3. Bake the shrimps for 15-20 minutes and set on wire rack to cool for 5 minutes.
4. Reheat the cabbage in microwave for 40-50 seconds on high.

5. Pour the melted butter sauce over the shrimps and cabbage before serving.

Horseradish Tilapia Cakes

Serves: 6 (6x2)

Preparation time: 25 min.

Cooking time: 8 min.

Ingredients:

- 2 lb. tilapia fillets
- 2 ½ tablespoons olive oil
- 2 eggs
- ½ cup mayonnaise
- 3 tablespoons horseradish
- Juice from 2 lemons
- ½ cup chopped parsley
- 36 saltine crackers, ground to get 1 ½ cup
- Fresh ground salt and pepper

Preparation method:

1. Preheat oven to 200C/400F and brush two baking sheets with olive oil.
2. Place tilapia fillets onto baking tray and season with salt and pepper.
3. Bake for 15 minutes and set on wire rack to cool completely.
4. When cooled, use a fork to flake the fish.
5. In a large bowl combine mayonnaise, eggs, parsley lemon juice and horseradish.
6. Stir in the flaked fish and ½ saltine crackers.
7. Season with salt and pepper and stir well to combine.
8. Form 12 cakes and gently roll them in the remaining crumbled crackers.

Freezing method:

1. Place the tilapia cakes in the food container, lined with parchment paper and set in the freezer. Keep until ready to use.

Cooking method:

1. Place the container with the cakes in a bowl filled with hot water for 5 minutes.
2. Heat some oil in non-stick pan over medium-high heat and cook the cakes for 6-8 minutes per side.
3. Set on paper towel and sprinkle with lemon juice before serving.

Simple Salmon Loaf

Serves: 6

Preparation time: 10 min.

Cooking time: 30 min.

Ingredients:

- 4 lb. can salmon, flaked
- ½ cup chopped fresh parsley
- 4 tablespoons butter, melted
- 2 cups potato chips, crushed
- 4 eggs, whisked
- 1 teaspoon red pepper flakes

Preparation method:

1. Combine all ingredients in a large bowl.
2. Divide into two loaf pans and wrap with parchment paper.

Freezing method:

1. Place the salmon loaf in the freezer and keep until ready to use.

Cooking method:

1. Set the salmon loaf in the refrigerator overnight to thaw.
2. Preheat oven to 200C/400F and place the salmon loafs onto baking tray lined with parchment paper.
3. Drizzle with olive oil and bake for 30 minutes.
4. Remove from the oven and cool slightly before serving.

Orange Salmon with Veggies

Serves: 6

Preparation time: 10 min.

Cooking time: 10 min.

Ingredients:

- 2 ½ lb. salmon fillets
- 2 tablespoons tablespoon teriyaki sauce
- ½ cup maple syrup
- 1 cup fresh squeezed orange juice
- 2 teaspoons orange zest
- ½ teaspoon lime zest
- 3 cups asparagus, cut into 2-inch pieces
- 2 cups onion, chopped

Preparation method:

1. In a small bowl combine orange zest, lime zest, orange juice, teriyaki sauce and maple syrup.
2. Place salmon fillets and veggies in a zip-lock bag and pour in prepared mixture.
3. Shake well until salmon and veggies are coated.

Freezing method:

1. Place the salmon in the flat position and freeze; keep until ready to use.

Cooking method:

1. Set the salmon and veggies in the refrigerator overnight to thaw.
2. Preheat grill pan and bake salmon, skin side down, for 10-12 minutes or just until salmon starts to flakes. Remove the salmon from the pan and add some oil. Cook vegetables for 2 minutes, stirring constantly.
3. Serve over salmon while still warm.

Creole Shrimps with Couscous

Serves: 6

Preparation time: 10 min.

Cooking time: 11 min.

Reheating time: 25 min.

Ingredients:

- 2 lb. cooked shrimps
- 3 tablespoons vegetable oil
- 1 onion, chopped
- 1 red bell pepper, chopped
- 3 garlic cloves, minced
- 14 oz. can diced tomatoes
- 8 oz. tomato sauce
- 1 tablespoon hot sauce
- 2 teaspoons sugar
- 2 teaspoons celery salt

- ¼ teaspoon cayenne pepper
- 2 tablespoon chopped parsley

For the couscous:

- 2 cups vegetable stock
- 1 ½ cups couscous
- Large pinch of salt

Preparation method:

1. Heat vegetable oil in the medium size pan and when it starts to simmer, add onion and bell pepper. Sauté for 10 minutes or until tender, over medium heat.
2. Add garlic and cook for 1 minute or until it becomes very fragrant.
3. Add remaining ingredients, stir well to combine and remove from the heat.
4. Set aside to cool.
5. Meanwhile prepare the couscous; bring the vegetable stock to boil over medium-high heat.
6. Stir in the couscous; remove from the heat and let it stand for 5 minutes.
7. Flake with the fork and set aside to cool.

Freezing method:

1. Pour the mixture, with shrimps into zip-lock freezer bags and set in freezer, in a flat position. Keep until ready to use and do the same with the couscous.

Reheating method:

1. Place the zip-lock bag in the refrigerator overnight to thaw.
2. Place the shrimps, with sauce in medium sauce pan and heat until it starts to simmer.
3. Simmer for 20 minutes and serve while still hot.
4. Reheating couscous; let it thaw overnight in refrigerator. Place couscous in the pan and add ¼ cup of vegetable stock. Reheat for 5 minutes over medium-high heat. Serve with shrimps.

Spicy Red Snapper with Cooked Rice

Serves: 6

Preparation time: 10 min.

Cooking time: 10 min.

Ingredients:

- 6 red snapper fillets, medium size
- 3 tablespoons teriyaki sauce
- 1 teaspoon red pepper flakes
- ¼ teaspoon chili powder
- 6 tablespoons lemon juice
- 6 tablespoons olive oil
- 2 cups cooked rice
- ½ cup grated parmesan

Preparation method:

1. Place the teriyaki sauce, lemon juice, spices and oil in food processor.
2. Pulse until well combined.

Freezing method:

1. Place the red snapper fillets in zip-lock freezer bags and pour in prepared mixture.
2. Seal the bag and shake well, so fish fillets are coated.
3. Place in the freezer; flat position.

Cooking method:

1. Set the salmon fillets into refrigerator overnight to thaw.
2. Place the red snapper fillets on broiler pan, skin side down.
3. Broil for 8-10 minutes, 6-inches from heat or until fish starts to flake.
5. Serve while still hot with cooked rice and sprinkle over grated parmesan.

Seafood Chowder

Serves: 6

Preparation time: 10 min.

Cooking time: 15 min.

Reheating time: 25 min.

Ingredients:

- 3 medium potatoes, peeled and diced
- 1 carrot, finely chopped
- 1 celery stalk, finely chopped
- 4 cups chicken or fish stock
- 1 ½ cup corn kernels
- 1 ¼ lb. marinara seafood mix
- 1 cup thickened cream
- 2 tablespoons chopped chives
- 2 tablespoons chopped parsley
- Fresh ground salt and pepper –to taste

Preparation method:

1. Place potatoes, carrot, stock and celery in a large pan.
2. Cover and bring to boil; reduce heat and simmer for 10 minutes.
3. Remove from the heat and using hand blender, mix until smooth.
4. Add corn kernels to the soup and simmer again for 10 minutes.
5. Reduce the heat and add seafood mix and cream.
6. Stir and cook, without boiling for 5 minutes or until seafood is cooked.
7. Season to taste and add chives and parsley.
8. Set aside to cool.

Freezing method:

1. Pour the cooled chowder in airtight container and place in the freezer; keep until ready to use.

Reheating method:

1. Place the airtight container in the bowl filled with hot water.
2. Transfer the chowder to the pot and heat over medium heat.
3. Stir the stew, gently to distribute heat evenly, but do not press because you may break the seafood and end up with the mush.
4. Bring stew to boil (you will need 25 minutes) and remove from the heat.
5. Serve immediately.

Pork Freezer Meals

Pork Casserole

Serves: 6

Preparation time: 10 min.

Cooking time: 57 min.

Ingredients:

- 3 cups diced ham
- 4 green onions, chopped
- 4 eggs, whisked
- 15 oz. creamed corn
- 12 oz. Mexican corn
- 8 oz. corn muffin mix
- 2 cups shredded cheddar cheese
- 1 ½ sticks butter, melted

Preparation method:

1. Combine all ingredients, except cheese in a large bowl.

2. Pour into foil pan, cover with plastic foil and with aluminum foil.
3. Place the shredded cheese in another zip-lock bag and set in the freezer.

Freezing method:

1. Set in the freezer, flat position and keep until ready to use.

Cooking method:

1. Place the casserole ingredients in a refrigerator or overnight to thaw.
2. Grease oven proof baking dish (7x11) and transfer the casserole ingredients in the dish.
3. Bake in preheated oven at 180C/356F for 55 minutes.
4. Sprinkle with cheese and bake for 2 minutes more.
5. Serve while still hot

Pork Tenderloin with Beer

Serves: 6

Preparation time: 10 min.

Cooking time: 18 min.

Ingredients:

- 2 pork tenderloins, about 12 oz. each
- ½ cup non-alcoholic beer
- 1/3 cup lemon juice
- 3 garlic cloves, minced
- 2 tablespoons chopped fresh parsley
- ½ teaspoon ground cumin
- ¼ teaspoon chili flakes
- ½ teaspoon chili powder
- Fresh ground salt and pepper

Preparation method:

1. In a large bowl whisk lemon juice, beer, spices, parsley, cumin and garlic.
2. Add pork and turn couple times to coat.

Freezing method:

1. Place the pork tenderloin in two zip-lock freezer bags.
2. Set in the freezer and keep up to a month or until ready to use.

Cooking method:

1. Place the tenderloin in refrigerator overnight to thaw.
2. Place pork on preheated grill over medium high heat and brush with some marinade.
3. Close with the lid and cook, flipping occasionally for 18 minutes.
4. Transfer to the cutting board and cover with aluminum foil; let it rest for 5 minutes before slicing.

Mustard Pork Chops with Applesauce

Serves: 6

Preparation time: 15 min.

Cooking time: 25 min.

Ingredients:

- 6 pork chops, boneless
- ½ cup honey
- 2 teaspoons Dijon mustard
- Fresh ground salt and pepper

For the apple sauce:

- 2 ½ cups apple sauce
- ¼ cup brown sugar
- ¼ teaspoon cinnamon
- 1 teaspoon ground mustard
- 1 small onion, thinly sliced

- Fresh ground salt and pepper

Preparation method:

1. Combine mustard and honey in a bowl and add salt and pepper.
2. Stir well to combine.
3. Place the pork chops in the freezer dish and top with mustard mixture.
4. Cover tightly with aluminum foil and place in the freezer.
5. Combine the apple sauce, onion, cinnamon, ground mustard and salt and pepper in a bowl.

Freezing method:

1. Place the freezer dish with pork chops in the freezer and keep up to 1 month or until ready to use. Place the apple sauce in another zip-lock bag.

Cooking method:

1. Place the pork chops and apple sauce in refrigerator overnight to thaw.
2. Preheat oven to 220C/425F.
3. Arrange pork chops onto rimmed baking tray and pour over thawed apple sauce; bake pork chops for 25 minutes.
4. Serve while still hot.

Spicy Pork Soup

Serves: 6

Preparation time: 5 min.

Cooking time: 25 min.

Reheating time: 22 min.

Ingredients:

- 1 lb. ground pork
- 3 garlic cloves, minced
- 3 teaspoons finely grated ginger
- ½ teaspoon crushed red pepper flakes
- 6 cups chicken stock
- 4 scallions, finely sliced
- 3 tablespoons soy sauce
- 10 oz. rice noodles
- 2 tablespoons vegetable oil
- 5 cups mustard greens
- Fresh ground salt and pepper
- 1 teaspoon cumin seeds

Preparation method:

1. Combine pork, cumin, red pepper flakes and ginger in a large bowl.
2. Heat oil in large pot over medium high heat.
3. Add pork mixture and season with salt and pepper.
4. Cook for 8-10 minutes or until browned.
5. Add stock and bring to boil; reduce heat to medium and simmer for 8-10 minutes.
6. Add scallions, soy sauce and cook for 5 minutes.
7. Season additionally with salt and pepper.

Freezing method:

1. Pour the cooled soup in zip-lock bags and place in the freezer, flat position.
2. Keep in the freezer until ready to use.

Reheating method:

1. Place the zip-lock bag with the soup in a bowl filled with hot water.
2. Let it sit for 5-7 minutes and transfer to the pot.
3. Heat over medium heat, stirring occasionally to distribute the heat.
4. Cook for 15 minutes and stir in torn mustard greens and rice noodles.
5. Cook additionally for 5-7 minutes and serve while still hot.

Pork Pies

Serves: 6

Preparation time: 15 min.

Cooking time: 35 min.

Ingredients:

- 1 ¼ lb. pork sausages
- 1 apple, grated
- 2 ¼ cups plain flour
- 1 egg, whisked
- 1 egg yolk, whisked
- 2 tablespoons butter
- 1 tablespoon chopped parsley
- ¼ teaspoon ground nutmeg
- Fresh ground salt and pepper
- ½ cup water

Preparation method:

1. Squeeze sausage meat from the casings into a bowl.
2. Add grated apple, nutmeg, parsley and season with salt and pepper.
3. Mix well to combine and set aside.
4. In separate bowl combine flour, pinch of salt with water and melted butter.
5. Add whisked egg and continue mixing with hands until you have a smooth ball.
6. Roll the dough onto floured surface and using cookie cutter, cut out 6 rounds from the dough.
7. Place the rounds into greased muffin tin, leaving slight overhang.
8. Divide the sausage meat between muffin holes.
9. Knead the remaining pastry and roll out once again; cut 6 more rounds and top the sausage meat.
10. Wrap with aluminum foil and freeze.

Freezing method:

1. Place the muffin tin in the freezer and keep until ready to use.

Cooking method:

1. Place the pork pies in refrigerator overnight to thaw.
2. Preheat oven to 200C/400F and brush pies with the whisked egg yolk. Sprinkle it with some coarse sea salt.
3. Bake the pies for 35 minutes or until golden. Set on wire rack to cool slightly before serving.

Pork Empanadas

Serves: 6

Preparation time: 20 min.

Cooking time: 30 min.

Ingredients:

- 1 lb. ground pork
- 2 tablespoons olive oil
- 2 teaspoons fresh sage
- 1 onion, diced
- 4 teaspoons flour
- 4 tablespoons water
- Fresh ground salt and pepper
- 2 garlic cloves, minced

For the pastry:

- 3 cups flour
- 2 teaspoons baking powder

- 1 ½ sticks butter, diced
- 1 egg
- 1 ¼ cup water, cold
- ½ teaspoon salt

Preparation method: Dough

1. Place sage, flour, baking powder and salt in food processor.
2. Pulse a couple of times and add butter; pulse a couple of times until you have mixture similar to coarse meal.
3. Add water and pulse again, until a ball forms. Transfer the dough to the floured kitchen surface and knead until it comes together.
4. Divide the dough in half and roll out on floured kitchen surface, until 1/8-inch thick.
5. Using a cookie cutter, 7-inch wide, cut out rounds. Knead the remaining dough, roll it out and continue cutting until you have 6 rounds.

Preparation method: The filling

1. Heat some oil in a large skillet and when hot add onion.
2. Cook for 10 minutes over medium-high heat and add garlic, pork and sage.
3. Mix in the flour and cook for 30 seconds.
4. Add 4 tablespoons of water and stir until thick.
5. Remove from the heat and season with salt and pepper.
6. Place 1/6 of the filling onto pastry, leaving a ½-inch border around the edge.
7. Brush the edges with water and fold the pastry over the filling. Pinch edges with fork.

Freezing method:

1. Place the empanadas on baking sheet and place into freezer, until firm.
2. Transfer to the airtight container and keep in the freezer until ready to use.

Cooking method:

1. Preheat oven to 200C/400F and line baking tray with parchment paper.
2. Brush empanadas with some vegetable oil or whisked egg yolk and arrange ½-inch apart on baking sheet.
3. Bake for 30 minutes or until golden.

Vegetarian Freezer Meals

Quinoa Cakes

Serves: 6

Preparation time: 7 min.

Cooking time: 10 min.

Reheating time: 90 sec.

Ingredients:

- 1 ½ cups quinoa
- 2 eggs, whisked
- ½ tablespoon garlic, minced
- 2 tablespoons flour
- 1 tablespoon olive oil
- 2 tablespoons shallots, diced
- 2 tablespoons breadcrumbs
- Fresh ground salt and pepper
- 3 tablespoons shredded Parmesan cheese
- Fresh salad – to serve

Preparation method:

1. Place all ingredients in a bowl, except olive oil, and let it stand for 5 minutes.
2. Form 6 patties and cook in heated olive oil in large pan, 5 minutes per side.
3. Place on paper towels to drain.

Freezing method:

1. Wrap the cooked patties in the parchment paper and place in airtight container.
2. Freeze until ready to use.

Reheating method:

1. Place the patties in microwave and heat on medium-high for 90 seconds. Serve with some fresh salad.

Rice Herbs and Cheese Balls

Serves: 6

Preparation time: 10 min.

Cooking time: 10 min.

Reheating time: 20 min.

Ingredients:

- 2 cups cooked rice, warm
- 2 eggs
- 1 ½ cups breadcrumbs
- 3 tablespoons grated parmesan cheese
- 1 tablespoon chopped parsley
- 1 teaspoon dried thyme
- 1 teaspoon dried sage
- 2 teaspoons dried basil
- Fresh ground salt and pepper – to taste
- 28 oz. tomato sauce

Preparation method:

1. Whisk the eggs, fresh ground salt, pepper, parsley and cheese.
2. Stir the egg mixture into warm rice and set aside to cool. Stir in the remaining herbs.
3. Form balls from the prepared mixture and coat them into breadcrumbs.
4. Heat oil in a nonstick skillet over medium heat. Cook the meatballs in the oil for 8-10 minutes, turning carefully, until light golden brown.
5. Drain meatballs on paper towels. Gently mix meatballs with tomato sauce.

Freezing method:

1. Place the rice balls, with sauce in zip-lock bag and freeze in flat position.

Reheating method:

1. Set the rice balls in refrigerator overnight, to thaw.

2. Place the rice balls in a saucepan and heat over medium low heat, stirring occasionally, until meatballs are hot all the way through, for 20 min.
3. Serve with some spaghetti.

Eggplant Lasagna

Serves: 6

Preparation time: 30 min.

Cooking time: 1 h. 10 min.

Ingredients:

- 1 ½ cup breadcrumbs
- 2 eggs, whisked with 1 tablespoon water
- 0.8 oz. grated Parmesan cheese
- 2 eggplants, medium size, cut into ½-inch rounds
- Fresh ground salt and pepper

Filling:

- ¼ cup grated Parmesan cheese
- 12 oz. ricotta cheese
- 1 egg, whisked
- 20 oz. tomato sauce
- Fresh ground salt and pepper

- 3 garlic cloves, minced
- 7 oz. mozzarella cheese

Preparation method:

1. Combine bread crumbs and parmesan cheese in a shallow dish.
2. Dip the eggplant slices in the egg mixture, drain the excess and dip in the breadcrumbs to coat well.
3. Place onto lined baking tray and bake in preheated oven at 180C/356F for 30 minutes.
4. Set aside to cool; meanwhile prepare the filling.
5. Combine all the egg, fresh ground salt and pepper, minced garlic, ricotta and parmesan cheese.
6. Assembling; place some of the tomato sauce in the bottom of baking dish.
7. Layer half of the eggplant slices over tomato sauce and top with ¾ cup sauce. Spread half of the filling mixture and top with 1/3 of mozzarella slices.

8. Repeat the process ending with tomato sauce.

Freezing method:

1. Cover the baking dish with the aluminum foil and tightly wrap with plastic foil.
2. Set in the freezer and keep until ready to use.

Cooking method:

1. Place the eggplant lasagna in refrigerator overnight to thaw.
2. Preheat the oven to 180C/356F and bake the lasagna for 35-40 minutes.
3. Set on wire rack to cool before slicing.

NOTE: You can bake lasagna from frozen condition, but prolong baking for 10 minutes more.

Stuffed Peppers

Serves: 6

Preparation time: 15 min.

Cooking time: 36 min.

Ingredients:

- 6 red or green bell peppers
- 1 cup cooked rice
- 1 ½ cup cooked red lentils
- 1 cup yellow onion, chopped
- 2 cups chopped spinach
- 1 tablespoon vegetable oil
- 3 garlic cloves, minced
- 1 teaspoon ground cumin
- 1 teaspoon tomato puree
- Fresh ground salt and pepper

Preparation method:

1. Heat oil in medium pan and when hot add onion; cook for 5 minutes; add garlic, cumin, tomato puree and cook further for 1 minute.
2. Add the lentils, rice and season with salt and pepper.
3. Stir in the chopped spinach; cook for 1 minute and remove from the heat.
4. Cut the tops from the pepper and remove the seeds.
5. Carefully cut the bottom of the peppers, so they can stand upright.
6. Fill each bell pepper with prepared mixture.

Freezing method:

1. Wrap the bell peppers in parchment paper and place in the freezer bags.
2. Set in the freezer and keep until ready to use.

Cooking method:

1. Set the peppers in refrigerator overnight to thaw.

2. Preheat the oven to 200C/400F and grease baking dish with some oil.
3. Place the peppers, upright, in the baking dish and bake for 30 minutes.
4. Serve with some toasted bread.

Vegetable Stew

Serves: 6

Preparation time: 30 min.

Cooking time: 3 min.

Reheating time: 20 min.

Ingredients:

- 3 zucchinis
- 2 eggplants
- 2 green peppers
- 4 tomatoes, large and ripe, peeled
- 1 tablespoon chopped basil
- Fresh ground salt and pepper
- 2 brown onions, medium
- 3 garlic cloves, minced
- 4 tablespoons vegetable oil
- 1 spring thyme – leaves only
- 1 tablespoon red wine vinegar
- 1 cup vegetable stock

Preparation method:

1. Chop eggplants and zucchinis in 2-inch slices; season with salt and pepper and set in colander for 30 minutes. Press veggies with a plate.
2. Meanwhile chop the peppers and onion; set aside.
3. To peel the tomatoes; make the "x" sign on the bottom of tomatoes. Place them in the pot with boiling water for 20 seconds and transfer them into ice cold water for 10 seconds.
4. Using a knife peel the tomatoes and remove the seeds; chop roughly.
5. Heat olive oil in large pot and add onion and garlic. Cook over medium heat for 5 minutes, stirring frequently. Add vegetable stock and bring to boil. Reduce heat to medium and cook for 2 minutes more.
6. Add drained eggplants.
7. Add basil and season with salt and pepper.
8. Cover the pot and simmer the veggies for 20 minutes.

9. Add the tomatoes and vinegar; cook for 5 minutes more. Stir in the zucchinis and cook for 5 minutes.
10. Set aside to cool.

Freezing method:

1. Place the veggies in airtight container and set in the freezer.
2. Keep until ready to use.

Reheating method:

1. Place frozen veggies in the large pot and add 2 tablespoons vegetable stock.
2. Heat over medium heat, slowly for 20 minutes.
3. Do not stir frequently because vegetables may become mushy.
4. Serve immediately.

Conclusion

I hope sincerely you enjoyed this book!

It is my deep desire that you enjoy a life full of energy and vitality!

Keep creating new recipes and having fun with the process!

Did you like this book?

If you enjoyed this book - please give your review on Amazon about it!

If you believe this book is worth sharing, would you take a few seconds to let your friends know about it? If it turns out to make a difference in their lives, they'll be forever grateful to you.

As I will.

All the best,

Morgan White

Other Books by Morgan White

Made in the USA
Middletown, DE
12 October 2014